Andre
Agassi

Tennis Prince

Gary Stern

ROURKE ENTERPRISES, INC.
VERO BEACH, FLORIDA 32964

A Blackbirch Graphics book.

Library of Congress Cataloging-in-Publication Data

Stern, Gary, 1949–
   Andre Agassi / by Gary Stern.
      p.   cm. — (The winning spirit)
   Includes index.
   Summary: A biography of the talented and colorful tennis player who won Wimbledon in 1992.
   ISBN 0-86592-055-9
   1. Agassi, Andre, 1970– —Juvenile literature. 2. Tennis players—United States—Biography—Juvenile literature. [1. Agassi, Andre, 1970– 2. Tennis players.] I. Title. II. Series.
GV994.A43S74 1993
796.342′092—dc20
[B]   92-46191
                                                               CIP
                                                               AC

Contents

1

Child Wonder

"I do everything by extremes."

*B*y the time Andre Agassi was 22 years old, he was one of the world's top tennis players. He had won Wimbledon in 1992, one of the most important tennis tournaments in the world. He had also played very well in the finals of one U.S. Open and two French Open championships.

Andre Agassi is more than just a gifted tennis player. To many people, he has become a symbol of the rebel in sports. "I do everything by extremes," he said when he was 20 years old. He has long hair, which he sometimes wears in a ponytail. He dresses in cut-off denim shorts instead of white tennis clothes. He looks different from most players and he acts with style.

Opposite: In 1992, Andre Agassi won Wimbledon and became a true tennis superstar.

Off the tennis court, Andre is very different. Because of his religious beliefs, he does not smoke or drink. Although he is followed everywhere by adoring teenage girls, Amy Moss has been his only girlfriend since 1987. He is very close to his family. He lives near his mother and father, and his brother travels with him to every tournament. He has had the same coach for almost ten years. Loyalty is an important value to Andre.

Companies hire Andre to appear in their commercials. He advertises tennis rackets, sneakers, cameras, and many other products. He earns over two million dollars a year just for doing these commercials.

But how did Andre develop into a tennis champion at such a young age? Who influenced him? How did he dedicate himself to winning? What struggles did he overcome to become a champion?

A Father's Dream

Andre Agassi was born on April 29, 1970, to Mike and Elizabeth (Betty) Agassi. From the day Andre was born, his father dreamed about his son becoming a championship tennis player. And he did everything he could to turn that dream into a reality.

Mike Agassi loved tennis. Back in Iran, where he was born, Andre's father lived near an American mission church. There were two

Andre got much of his early love of tennis from his father. Here, young Andre (left) sits for a family portrait with his father, sister Rita, and older brother Phil.

tennis courts there. At the young age of eight, Mike was fascinated by watching American soldiers play tennis. Growing up, he worked on the court, watering it and keeping it in good shape for all the people who used it.

Mike Agassi moved to America and settled in Las Vegas, Nevada. The year-round warm climate of Las Vegas appealed to him. He chose Las Vegas because tennis could be played there nearly every day of the year.

When Andre was born, Mike and Betty already had a son and a daughter. During the day, Mike worked as a showroom captain at Caesars Palace hotel. After work, he would spend most of his time on the tennis court, teaching his children the game.

Andre started playing tennis at the earliest age of all the Agassi children. Mike placed a tennis ball at the top of Andre's crib. He wanted Andre to begin to wonder about tennis. He thought that Andre would play with the ball over his crib and that this would help his timing and coordination. By the age of two, Mike Agassi swears that Andre could serve on the tennis court.

An Unforgettable Experience

At age four, young Andre had an experience that he would recall later in his life. The best tennis player of his day, Jimmy Connors, was in Las Vegas. He was introduced to Mike. Mike

Andre had a tennis racket in his hand almost from the time he could walk. Here, about age five, Andre works on his serving technique.

convinced Jimmy to hit tennis balls with young Andre. Fifteen years later, Andre would be playing Jimmy again, but this time in a professional match.

Andre's First Teacher

At the age of six, Andre was learning the secrets of tennis. His father was teaching him certain techniques that would one day make him a champion. For example, his father taught him to hit the ball early. By hitting the ball on the rise, Andre could hit it harder and on a better angle. This remains one of Andre's main strengths in tennis today.

Back then, Mike Agassi was training Andre to become a champion. "Don't just try to get the ball in," he would tell him. "Smack the ball. Crunch it. Hit it as hard as you can. We'll worry about keeping it in later."

To improve Andre's return of serve, his father saved up $860 to buy a ball machine (a machine that automatically returns balls on the court). He placed the machine at one end of the court. It would send balls at 100 miles per hour at Andre. At first, it was quite frustrating for the young Andre to try to return the ball across the net. But the practice and hard work paid off in the end. Today, Andre's return of serve is one of the strongest and fiercest in the game, and one of his main skills as a tennis player.

A Champion at Seven

At age seven, Andre entered his first tennis tournament. It was for players under 10 years of age. He won the first nine tournaments he entered. Sometimes, his mother drove him 500 miles to southern California to the tournaments. By age 13, Andre was beating everyone. There was no one left for him to play or beat. Andre was becoming very restless. He was losing interest in school and was not being challenged in tennis.

One Sunday night, Mike Agassi was sitting at home watching the television show "60 Minutes." There was a segment on a very special tennis school for youngsters, the Nick Bollettieri Tennis Academy, located in Bradenton, Florida. Gifted young tennis players were sent to this academy to master the game. Nick Bollettieri was one of the most talented tennis teachers in the world. Top-ten tennis players like Jimmy Arias and Aaron Krickstein studied with Nick. Mike Agassi knew that he had to send Andre to this special academy to improve his game.

2

The Tennis Academy

*"I didn't know what I'd do if I had to work
eight hours a day in a typical job."*

Mike Agassi decided to send his son
thousands of miles away to Nick Bollettieri's
Tennis Academy to make sure he would receive
the best tennis teaching in the world. Mike
figured that he had done everything possible
for Andre's tennis game. Now it was time for
Nick Bollettieri and his team of pros to improve
his son's special skills.

Andre was involved in the decision to leave
home at age 13 to study at Nick's academy. He
was eager to become a professional tennis
player. "I didn't know what I'd do if I had to
work eight hours a day" in a typical job, says
Andre. He wanted to go to the academy and
he wanted to improve his tennis game so he
could become a tennis pro.

*Opposite: By the age of seven, Andre was already winning amateur
tennis tournaments.*

But like any 13-year-old boy, Andre was nervous about leaving home. He was afraid that the academy would be very strict, have many rules, and would limit his freedom. In 1983, he packed his bags, kissed his parents, sister, and brother, good-bye, and headed for Bradenton, Florida.

Life at Nick's Camp

The academy was not the prison Andre had imagined it would be. On the contrary, Andre felt like he had been sent to a giant summer camp. Students lived in dormitory rooms like college students. They were sent to school in the morning, but returned to the tennis academy by one o'clock to be taught tennis. Over 175 junior tennis players from all over the United States, Europe, Latin America, and Asia boarded at Nick's academy. They all played tennis in a complex of 67 courts and ate all their meals in a big cafeteria, as if they were students attending college.

Andre Gets a Scholarship

The cost for staying at the Bollettieri Academy was about $20,000 a year. That was a lot of money for Mike, the showroom captain of a Las Vegas hotel. But Nick was so impressed with Andre's playing and his high junior ranking that he gave Andre a full scholarship. His father would not have to pay anything.

Andre had lots of freedom at the Academy—too much freedom. He started to break rules. He was not listening to the pros and he played jokes on his fellow tennis players. In his words, "I was just so obnoxious."

A Behavior Problem

The camp liked to stress discipline on and off the court. Andre refused to follow rules. He was very rude on the tennis court. He hated losing. He couldn't stand it. Faced with losing, he would throw his tennis racket on the court, smashing it to pieces. He had a bad temper. In one match he smashed seven tennis rackets. The tennis instructors felt that he had an "attitude problem" and figured that he would never make it as a pro or last at the academy.

From ages 13 to 15, Andre was not one of the stars of Nick's academy. He would win a match, then lose several matches. His anger and his tantrums on the court distracted him. Living up to his father's demanding expectations caused him to be moody and nervous.

Just for fun one day, Andre shaved his hair and got a Mohawk haircut. He also played one tournament in Florida wearing jeans, lipstick, eyeliner, and an earring. Nick was furious with him. He criticized him in front of the other tennis players. Andre was angry. He returned to his room and packed his bags. He had decided to go back home to Las Vegas.

Nick did not want him to leave. Andre started walking to the airport. Later, he calmed down and returned to the academy. He told Nick that he had to talk with him. "You people don't realize how tough it is on kids," he told him. At age 15, Andre was already facing the intense pressure to win at tennis, to beat all of his opponents, to keep his ranking high. Andre reminded Nick that he was still a kid, not a tennis pro. Nick sat and listened to him and began to understand how much pressure the 15-year-old Andre was facing.

Playing Against a Pro

By this time he had been playing in amateur junior tennis tournaments for five years. Though still an amateur, he entered his first tournament and played a tennis pro from Yugo-slavia named Marko Ostoja. The tournament was a small one in which players had to make their own line calls (decide whether a ball is inside or outside the line). There were no refer-ees. To upset his opponent, Andre called a ball out that was clearly in.

His opponent reached across the net and slapped him hard. Andre was upset, but the linesman did not punish his opponent. Andre was so angry that he lost his concentration and lost the match. Andre was beginning to realize that he would have to change his behavior in order to beat tennis pros.

Andre was itching to turn pro. It costs money to buy rackets and shoes, travel to tennis tournaments, stay at hotels, and eat in restaurants. Nick used his connections to gain Andre a contract from Nike, a sports shoe company. The company would pay Andre about $25,000. In return, he agreed to wear Nike sneakers in all of his tournaments. That money allowed Andre to turn pro and play in all of the major tennis competitions.

3

On the Pro Tour
"...It's no big deal if you get beat."

*O*n May 1, 1986, two days after his sixteenth birthday, Andre turned professional. He started entering the satellite tournaments (small tournaments held around the world). He was five feet eleven inches tall and weighed 150 pounds. Most of the pros weighed more than Andre, and they were stronger. Andre was not yet physically mature enough to win.

In his first two professional tournaments, Andre did very well. He won $11,500—and made the finals of one tournament. Andre had risen from number 618 to the 211th best tennis player in the world. Then the pressure started getting to him.

Andre's Coach

From April 1986 through April 1987, Andre won only two matches. By the time he lost in the first round of a tournament in Washington, he was thinking of quitting. Andre said, "I was ready to pack it in for the summer. Nothing seemed to be working. My attitude was shot." But his coach helped him to hang in.

Nick Bollettieri had been with him since Andre was 13 years old and he continued to be his coach when Andre turned pro. He eventually gave up coaching famous tennis players to work full-time with Andre.

Nick and Andre got along well. As Nick once said, "I relate well to Andre. He's a character, and I'm a character. He's fun, generous, sympathetic. He's my friend."

Nick was once asked if it was difficult to coach Andre. Nick replied, "Andre is a real individualist. Nobody is going to tell him what to do, although he'll listen to the people he trusts. . . . The strain was starting to show when Andre came to us. If Andre didn't come to us, he might have quit tennis altogether."

Nick had a long-range plan for Andre. He knew that Andre would suffer losses on his way to winning. In one tournament in Rome, Andre lost to Claudio Panatta. Andre could have won the match, but he was impatient. The match was played on clay, and the ball moves rather slowly on this surface. Andre tried to finish points too quickly rather than wait for the right opportunities. After the match, Andre felt very depressed. In his diary of his first year on tour, published in *Tennis* magazine, Andre wrote, "If you want to be a clay-courter, you have to discipline yourself, play matches, and not get depressed, not get down on yourself. Learning to play on clay will help a player's mental discipline."

A New Attitude

Andre stayed on the tour in 1987. He started winning more matches than he had in his first year. Then he entered the Stratton Tennis Tournament in Stratton, Vermont. After deciding that he wanted more than anything in the world to become a successful pro player, he adopted a new attitude. He wanted to have fun on the court and not concern himself with winning and losing.

He played another young tennis pro, Luke Jensen, in the opening round. Jensen won the first set, yet Andre was applauding Jensen's winning passing shots. He decided not to put pressure on himself. He was starting to enjoy tennis, and he did well. He beat Jensen and won the next two matches. One tennis writer noted that at that match Andre stopped acting in a self-destructive way. Now he would focus all of his energy on beating his opponents, not on destroying himself.

Andre poses for a formal portrait with some of his closest and most important friends. From left to right: Manager Bill Shelton, Coach Nick Bollettieri, and brother Phil.

Andre's trainer, Gil Reyes (left), and Andre's brother Phil have both been great sources of support for the tennis star.

Agassi lost to John McEnroe, four-time winner of the U.S. Open, in the quarterfinals. After that match, John said, "No one's ever hit the ball that hard against me." Even at that early point in Andre's career, John was able to notice the stuff of champions. "He's still a kid, but he has that confidence, the attitude, the feeling of a champion," said John. Andre ended the year ranked number 91, but he was not satisfied to set his sights on anything less than number 1.

Balancing His Life Through Religion

Part of what kept Andre going and believing in himself was his religion. Andre is a practicing Christian who reads the Bible every day. The Bible is his favorite book. Andre belives that religion keeps his entire life in focus and in

balance. Andre says, "there are only two direc-
tions in life, one that leads to helping others
and one that leads to selfish purposes. I wasn't
on my way to helping others. I was concerned
with myself. But what Christianity has offered
in my life is peace of mind and understanding
that it's no big deal if you get beat."

Help from Big Brother

Philip, Andre's 29-year-old brother, has also
played a major role in helping Andre become
a top tennis pro. Philip is Andre's personal

*In 1987, the world began to pay more attention to Andre Agassi.
Here, he signs autographs for fans after beating Jimmy Connors in
a Florida tournament.*

In 1987, Andre started to date Amy Moss. Since then, she has been his only serious female companion.

manager, traveling companion, and friend. Whenever Andre travels to a tournament, Philip is there at his side. Philip was once a satellite tennis pro, but he quit the game when Andre turned pro.

In the Grand Slam events (U.S. Open, French Open, Wimbledon, and Australian Open), where the pressure is very strong, Andre did not perform well in 1987. He lost in the second round at the French Open and in the first rounds of Wimbledon and the U.S. Open (both times to Henri Leconte, a French player).

It would take at least another year for Andre to gain the maturity to win matches at a Grand Slam event.

The World Takes Notice

On the tour in 1987, Andre started beating the other pros consistently. At a tournament in Amelia Island, Florida, he beat Jimmy Connors for the first time (the same tennis player whom he had hit with when he was four years old). He won a Grand Prix tournament in Brazil, and earned $90,000. At age 17, he became the youngest tennis player to win the Volvo U.S. Indoor held in Memphis, Tennessee. He beat Swedish player Mikael Pernfors in that match, winning $53,550 for that victory. Andre was quickly rising up the ranks of the tennis pros. By the end of 1987, he had become the 25th best tennis player in the world. People were now beginning to take notice of Andre Agassi.

4

A Banner Year

"He's a great showman and a great sportsman."

*A*ndre will never forget the year 1988. That was the year he became one of the world's top tennis players. Until then, he was just one of the many young tennis players who showed promise in the game. He hit the ball harder than most tennis players, but until 1988 he was never able to put everything together on the court. Twenty-four players in the world still ranked above him. Many players had risen to be in the top 25 and then faded.

In League with the Best

In 1988, Andre won six tennis titles. Mats Wilander, who was then the number one tennis player in the world, also won six. Andre thus

Opposite: Andre clowns with fellow tennis great Boris Becker.

tied with the world's top player for winning. All told, he won 62 matches and lost only 9 matches, a winning percentage of .873.

Tennis players usually make their lasting reputation at one of the four Grand Slam tournaments. Each of these tournaments attracts 128 players. The champion must win seven matches in two weeks to earn a victory. In two of the tournaments, Andre played against Boris Becker and Stefan Edberg. These two pros ranked among the top four tennis players in the world. When Andre beat them, he became the world's third best tennis player.

Making Changes

Other tennis players noticed the difference in Andre's game and approach to tennis. His archrival, top ten tennis player Jim Courier, said, "He did everything the same as ever, only better. His serve keeps improving." And tennis star Stefan Edberg commented, "Nobody pounds you like Andre. He beats you more in the legs than any other guy."

By the end of 1988, Andre had made it to the semifinals of the French Open. He lost to Mats Wilander in five sets. Mats eventually won the tournament. At the U.S. Open, he also made it to the semifinals. *Tennis* magazine named him the Most Improved Pro of 1988.

Speaking about 1988, his most successful year in tennis, Andre has said, "I have to keep

1988 was a great year for Andre Agassi. In addition to improving his world ranking, he was given the Most Improved Player of the Year award from the Association of Tennis Professionals and from Tennis magazine.

in perspective that getting to this point in my career has happened because I went out, number one, to enjoy myself. My priorities are to enjoy myself and not be concerned with winning or losing or with my ranking."

Andre also matured as a pro. "I had to go through some really bad times before I could start taking responsibility for myself. Now I'm playing for myself, and that's a big difference. I now know that if I stay positive and keep on working, my talent will eventually come out," he said.

He also decided to work harder and to become physically stronger in order to beat the top players in the world. He had his own physical-conditioning coach and each day he would spend long hours working on his tennis strokes on the court. In addition, he became involved in weight training to increase his strength. He did workouts to improve his movement and agility. He would also perform drills of running through rows of tires to increase his stamina.

Mr. Popularity

Andre quickly became one of the most popular players with the fans on the tour. At the French Open, he received more requests to be interviewed from journalists than any other player. Teenage girls treated him as if he were a rock star. They threw flowers at him and begged him for autographs. Whenever he tossed a pair of his denim shorts into the crowd, teenagers would grab for the prized possession. Writers and photographers followed him as if he were Liz Taylor, Tom Cruise, or Julia Roberts.

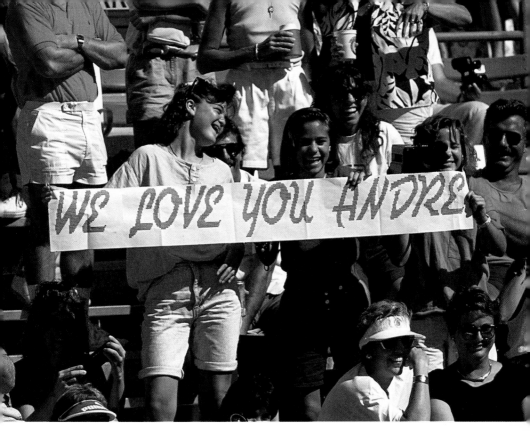

Andre has become one of the most personally popular players in professional tennis. Fans all over the world treat him like a movie star or teen idol.

When his sister Rita started the Andre Agassi Fan Club, Andre began to receive 2,000 letters a week. At the 1988 U.S. Open, 200 pairs of Andre Agassi tennis shorts sold out in two days. Now, Andre could no longer eat in a public restaurant without being mobbed by people who wanted his autograph.

Money from Commercials

Andre was also making a lot of money. In 1988, he earned $822,062 from his tennis victories, compared with about $300,000 in 1987. But he earned lot's more—about two million dollars—from companies that paid him to be a spokesperson for their products. Andre would use the products, like tennis rackets and sneakers, and then tell people in commercials how much he liked them. The companies figured that many tennis players would buy their products, thinking that they, too, could win. One tournament director and former tennis pro, Charlie Pasarell, explained Agassi's popularity by saying, "He creates a tremendous amount of enthusiasm in a stylish way. He's a great showman and a great sportsman."

Trying for a Grand Slam Win

After another successful year in 1989, there was only one more goal that Andre had in tennis: To win one of the Grand Slam tournaments. He had won many tournaments, earned millions of dollars, and become a teenage idol. He was known throughout the United States. But even with all this success, he had never won a Grand Slam tournament.

In July of 1990 at the French Open, Andre was ready for victory. The French Open is the only Grand Slam tournament played on clay, which is the slowest of all surfaces. It gives Andre the most time to hit winning shots. The players with powerful serves have a harder time on clay because it slows down their serve.

In the quarterfinals, Andre had to play against Michael Chang, another American.

Chang, who is a very tough opponent, is a year younger than Andre. In 1989, Chang had won the French Open, beating Ivan Lendl. Chang had great mental toughness and was very difficult to beat on clay. But that day, Andre was playing especially well. He won the first two sets 6-2, 6-1. Then Chang regained his touch and won the third set 6-4. Andre would not be denied. He beat Chang in the fourth set 6-2.

Andre was in the semifinals and one step closer to winning his first Grand Slam. If he could win the semifinals, then the finals, the championship would be his.

In the semifinals he was up against Jonas Svennson, a young up-and-coming Swedish player. Andre beat Jonas in four sets. Now came the last hurdle: the finals. Andre played Andres Gomez, a 30-year-old from Ecuador. Andres was in the top ten and had been on the mens' tour for years, but, like Andre, he had never won a Grand Slam tournament.

The Ecuadorian knew that Andre would be a tough opponent. He figured that Andre would try to outhit him in the match. But Andres decided that he would not play it safe at the French Open. "My game is not based on how many errors I make but on how many winners I make," Andres said later.

That day, everything was working for Andres. His serve was going in the corners and his forehands were hitting the line. "My head is clear. I am concentrating. Everything is clicking," Andres said about the match. "He was going for every shot, and it worked for him," said Andre.

Andres won the first set 6-2, but Andre tied the match, winning the second set 6-2. When Andres found himself getting a little tired, he pumped himself up and went for winning shots. He won both the third and fourth sets by 6-4. When they were done, the Ecuadorian had won the French Open. Andre would have to wait for another chance at a Grand Slam final.

Andre Loses the U.S. Open

In September of 1990, two months after losing the French Open, Andre tried for victory again, this time at the U.S. Open. Andre was in top form. In the quarterfinals, he beat Russian player Andrei Cherkasov, who is always a tough opponent and who likes to run down every shot. Still, Andre beat him in straight sets 6-2, 6-2, 6-3. Once again, Andre needed only two more victories for a Grand Slam trophy.

In the semifinals, Andre faced Boris Becker. Boris was a two-time winner of the Wimbledon championship. He had one of the toughest serves in the game. Boris fought to win the first set 12-10, in a tiebreaker. He appeared to be well on his way to making it to the finals. But then Andre won nine games when Boris was serving, which is not an easy task. But Boris's

Although Andre made it to the finals in two Grand Slam tournaments in 1990, both wins slipped away. During that year, Andre began to wonder if he would ever win a big title.

mean serve was not on target that day, and
Agassi won the next three sets 6-3, 6-3, 6-2.

In the finals, Andre played 20-year-old Pete
Sampras. At the beginning of the year, Pete
ranked only 81 and had won just two tournaments as a pro. Most experts figured that Andre
would most probably be the winner. He had
already been to a Grand Slam final, had more
experience with the pressure, and was a higher-
ranked player.

Tennis magazine wrote that "there was no
way Sampras was supposed to win the U.S.
Open." But Pete Sampras had a punishing
125-mile-per-hour serve. He had beaten two
Grand Slam winners—Ivan Lendl, in the
quarterfinals; and John McEnroe, in the semifinals—to earn his shot at the finals.

Pete was placing his serve wherever he
wanted. Even Andre, known as having one of
the best returns of serve in the game, had a
problem returning it. In fact, the match was not
very close. Pete waltzed to victory in straight
sets, 6-4, 6-3, 6-2.

Twice Andre had made it to a Grand Slam
final, and both times he had lost. He had won
seven matches to earn his place in the finals,
but he could not finish off Andres Gomez or
Pete Sampras. Sportswriters were beginning to
question whether he really had the stuff of a
true champion, as John McEnroe had predicted
several years ago.

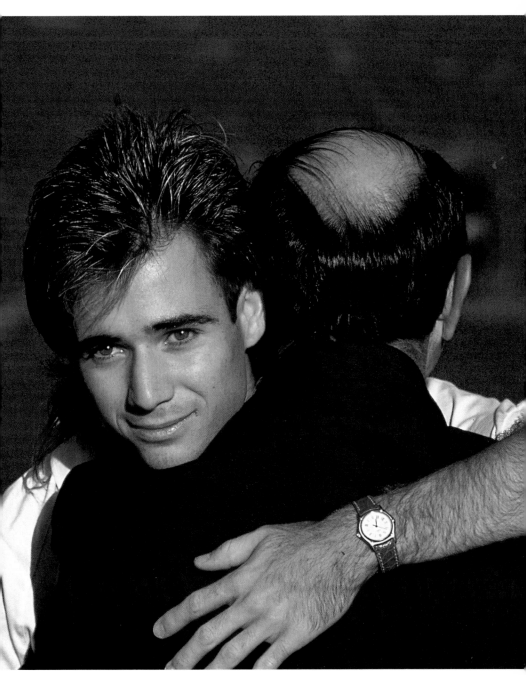

Andre has always relied on his father to provide him with strength, confidence, and support.

Another Loss at the French Open

At the 1991 French Open, Andre was again playing excellent tennis. In the early rounds, he beat Jacob Hlasek in straight sets 6-3, 6-1, 6-1 in just 75 minutes. In the semifinals, he faced Boris Becker. He had beaten Becker three times in a row. Andre won a very difficult first set 7-4 and then won the second set 6-3. Boris's serve led him to win the third set, but Andre easily won the fourth set 6-1.

For the third time in two years, Andre had made it to the finals of a Grand Slam match. But this time he would be facing his old friend and schoolmate, Jim Courier. Andre and Jim knew each other from the time they were students at the Bollettieri Tennis Academy.

On a nasty, rainy day in Paris on June 9, 1991, Andre came out in the first set and looked as if he were ready to win. He won the first set 6-3. He led 3-1 in the second set. Then it started to rain. The match was halted. This was a good time for Jim's coach to talk to him, since coaches cannot meet with players during a match. His coach told him that he noticed Andre was serving very well and deep into the court. He suggested that Jim stand two steps farther back on the court. The rain stopped, and Jim followed his coach's advice.

Jim won that second set 6-4. Andre won the third set. Jim, however, won the fourth and fifth sets, 6-1, 6-4. Jim had become the French

In 1991, Andre was part of the American Davis Cup team. His teammates were (left to right) Pete Sampras, Captain Tom Gorman, and doubles partners Ken Flash and Robert Seguso.

Open champion. After the match, Andre told the press that the rain delay turned the match around. "I felt like if it had not rained I could have kept my momentum" and won, he said. Would this third loss mean that Andre would never win a Grand Slam match?

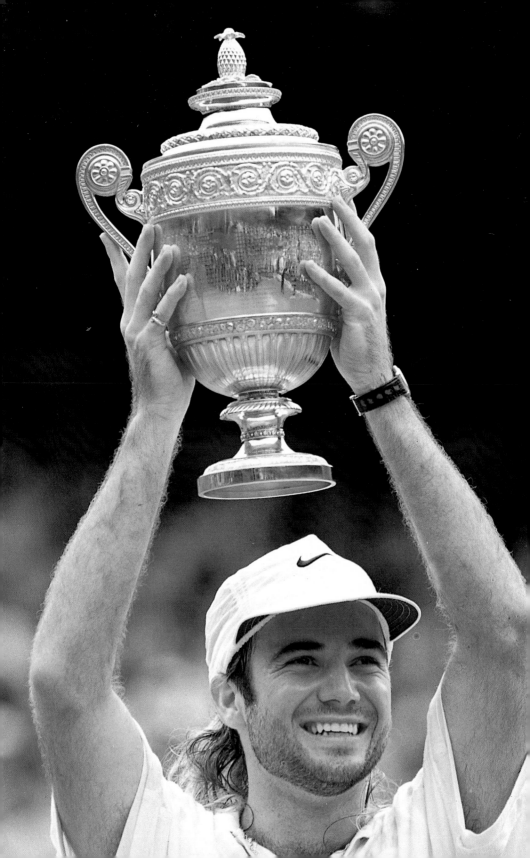

5

Winning Wimbledon
"I felt extremely relaxed and poised."

*B*efore the 1992 Wimbledon championship, some sportswriters were calling Andre
Agassi a loser. Three times he had made it to
the finals of a Grand Slam tournament, and
each time he had lost. Losing a Grand Slam
match in tennis is like making it to baseball's
World Series and losing. Only the winners are
remembered.

In the past, Andre had chosen not to play at
Wimbledon. Wimbledon is the only tournament played on grass. The others are played
on either clay or concrete courts. Grass courts
favor a player with a big serve. And many
players on the tour have serves that are faster
than Andre's.

*Opposite: In 1992, Andre proved to the world that he had what it
takes to be a true champion.*

The Quarterfinals

Andre easily won his first few matches. In the quarterfinals he had to play a German, Boris Becker. Boris had already won the Wimbledon championship twice before. Most experts predicted that Becker, with his big serve, would have no trouble beating Andre.

The first set went as expected. Becker won it 6-4. Few people gave Andre much of a chance, but he refused to give in. He came back and won the next two sets, 6-2, 6-2. Then Boris won the fourth set 6-4. The match was tied two sets each.

The Semifinals

Still determined to win, Andre beat Boris in the final set 6-3. This victory sent him into the semifinals to face the great American champion, John McEnroe. At 32 years old, John was not as quick as he had been ten years ago. In the semifinals, Andre had little trouble with him and he won the match easily in straight sets 6-4, 6-2, 6-3. Now, after all his hard work and determination, he was in the Wimbledon final.

A Dream Come True

His opponent was Gopran Ivaniscevic. Gopran had one of the most powerful serves on the mens' professional tour. His serve had been clocked at 130 miles per hour. It was very difficult to return.

Andre used every ounce of talent, training, and concentration that he had to win Wimbledon in 1992.

Winning Wimbledon was an emotional experience for Andre. After the final point, he put down his racket and wept tears of joy in front of a wildly cheering crowd.

Most people figured that Gopran would win. His serve would give him many aces (unreturnable serves) and set up many easy points. As expected, Gopran won the first set 7-6. But Andre had a weapon that few people

gave him enough credit for: his return of serve.
All of those days back in Las Vegas when his father would send serves off the ball machine were paying off. Andre won the second and third sets 6-4. But in the fourth set, Gopran bounced back and won 6-1. Now it was a match that would be determined by the winner of the fifth set.

Despite having lost three Grand Slams before, Andre felt unusually confident at this one. He said, "I felt extremely relaxed and poised. I felt an overflowing desire to go out there and hit shots."

With Andre leading 5-4 in the final set, Gopran was serving to tie the match. But he seemed to be feeling the pressure of being in a Grand Slam final, and he double-faulted twice (meaning his serves were not good and he lost two points) and lost the match 6-4.

Winning the match brought tears to Andre's eyes. No longer would anyone call him a loser. He had become the 1992 Wimbledon champion and that was something no one could ever take away from him. His father had always raised Andre to be a champion. Finally his dream had turned into a reality.

Glossary

ace (on service) A point earned on serving a ball that cannot be returned.

double fault When both serves land outside the serving box.

Grand Slam event U.S. Open, French Open, Australian Open, and Wimbledon tournaments.

linesperson An official of a tennis match whose duty it is to decide whether balls are inside or outside side lines and base lines.

satellite tournament Small tournaments held around the world.

semifinals The two matches played before the final round of a tournament.

set A number of games played for someone to be declared a winner.

For Further Reading

Bailey, Donna. *Tennis.* Austin: Raintree Steck-Vaughn, 1991.

Bollettieri, Nick, with McDermott, Barry. *Nick Bollettieri Junior Tennis.* New York: Simon & Schuster, 1984.

Gutman, Bill. *Tennis.* New York: Marshall Cavendish, 1990.

Wimbledon. Mankato, Minnesota: Creative Education, 1990.

Index

Photo Credits: